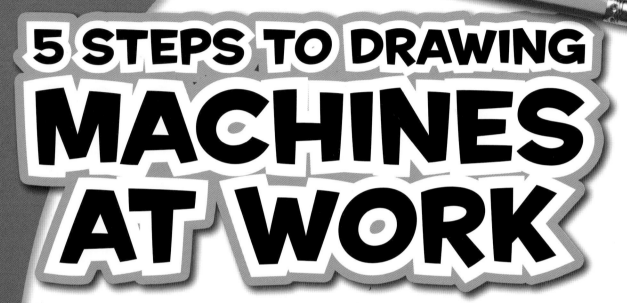

5 STEPS TO DRAWING
MACHINES
AT WORK

by Susan Kesselring • illustrated by Susan DeSantis

Published by The Child's World®
1980 Lookout Drive • Mankato, MN 56003-1705
800-599-READ • www.childsworld.com

ACKNOWLEDGMENTS
The Child's World®: Mary Berendes, Publishing Director
The Design Lab: Design and production
Red Line Editorial: Editorial direction

ISBN: 978-1-60973-201-1
LCCN: 2011927710

Printed in the United States of America
Mankato, MN
July 2011
PA02088

TABLE OF CONTENTS

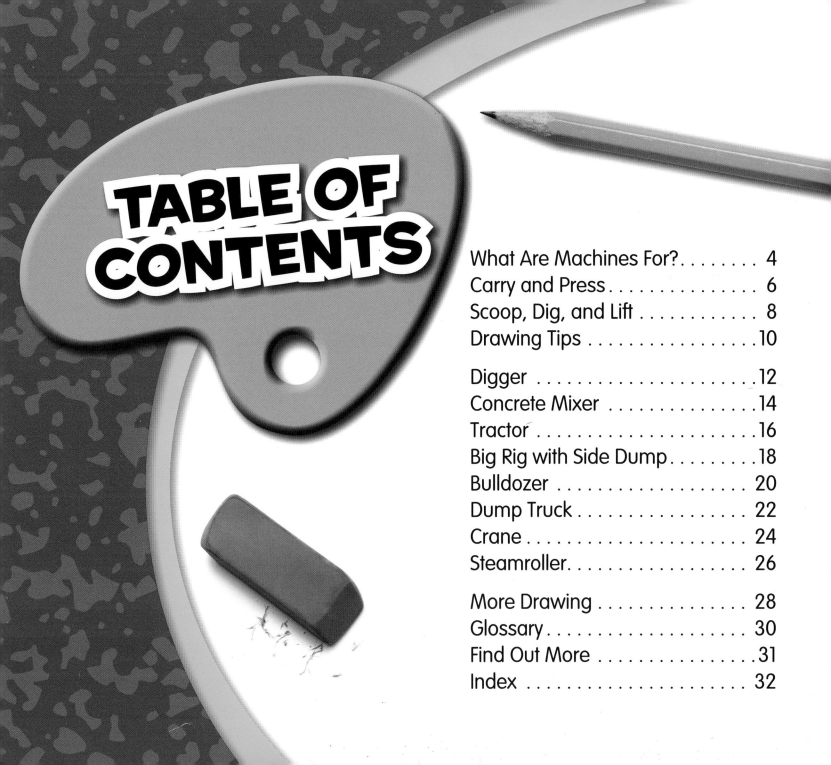

WHAT ARE MACHINES FOR?

People have been using machines for a long time. Ancient Greeks made the first cranes. People or donkeys powered these cranes. The first steamrollers were called road rollers. They were pulled by horses. Bulldozers were used as tanks in World War I. Today's machines are bigger and more powerful than ever. But they do many of the same things.

What would we do without machines? We wouldn't be able to build tall buildings or make roads. Farming would be much harder. Lifting heavy things would be hard to do. Carrying things like **concrete** from place to place would take a lot longer. Thankfully, we do have machines to help us with these things!

CARRY AND PRESS

Some machines are helpful for building things. Concrete mixers are important for making houses and buildings. They bring concrete to **construction sites**. Mixers have big tanks to carry the wet concrete. Each tank spins to mix the concrete. The turning also keeps the concrete from getting hard in the tank.

Dump trucks and big rigs with side dumps bring materials to construction sites, too. These trucks can hold lots of sand, gravel, and dirt. Some dump trucks can carry up to 60,000 pounds (27,216 kg)! Big rigs with side dumps can carry even more than dump trucks.

Machines do more than help us make buildings. We need machines to help us **pave** roads and sidewalks. Steamrollers help make the roads that people drive on. They move pretty slowly. But they do a big job. They press the gravel to make it smooth and packed down.

SCOOP, DIG, AND LIFT

Some machines help destroy old buildings. Then, new buildings can be built in their place. Diggers scoop up **rubble** after a building is knocked down. The top part of a digger can turn in a full circle. This way, the digger does not need to drive through a lot of rubble. Bulldozers can help clean up after a building is knocked down, too. Bulldozers can also dig and carry things.

Tractors are used for many jobs. Farmers use tractors for planting and picking crops. Tractors can even plow snow. Cranes are great for lifting heavy objects. They are often used to load and unload things from trucks or ships.

For every tough job, there is a mighty machine to help. Can you draw these helpful machines?

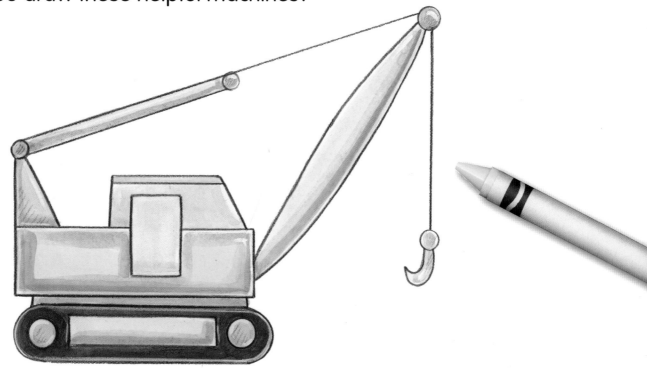

DRAWING TIPS

You've learned about machines at work. You're almost ready to draw them. But first, here are a few drawing tips:

Every artist needs tools. To learn how to draw machines, you will need:

- Some paper
- A pencil
- An eraser
- Markers, crayons, colored pencils, or watercolors (optional)

Anyone can learn to draw. You might think only some people can draw. That's not true. Everyone can learn to draw. It takes practice, though. The more you draw, the better you will be. With practice, you will become a true artist!

Everyone makes mistakes. This is okay! Mistakes help you learn. They help you know what not to do next time. Mistakes can even make your drawing more special. It's all right if you draw the wheels too big. Now you've got a one-of-a-kind drawing. You can erase a mistake you don't like, too. Then start again!

Stay loose. Relax your body before you begin. Hold your pencil lightly. Don't rest your wrist on the table. Instead, move your whole arm as you draw. This will help you make smooth lines. Press lightly on the paper when you draw or erase.

Drawing is fun! The most important thing about drawing is to have fun. Be creative. Your drawings don't have to look exactly like the pictures in this book. Try changing the size of the shovel or bucket. You can also use markers, crayons, colored pencils, or watercolors to bring your machines to life.

1

2

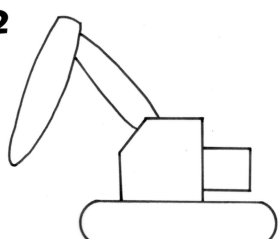

DIGGER

3

4

A digger is also known as a backhoe. It has a deep shovel attached to the front to scoop dirt. Some diggers have **treads** instead of wheels. Treads keep the diggers from getting stuck in dirt.

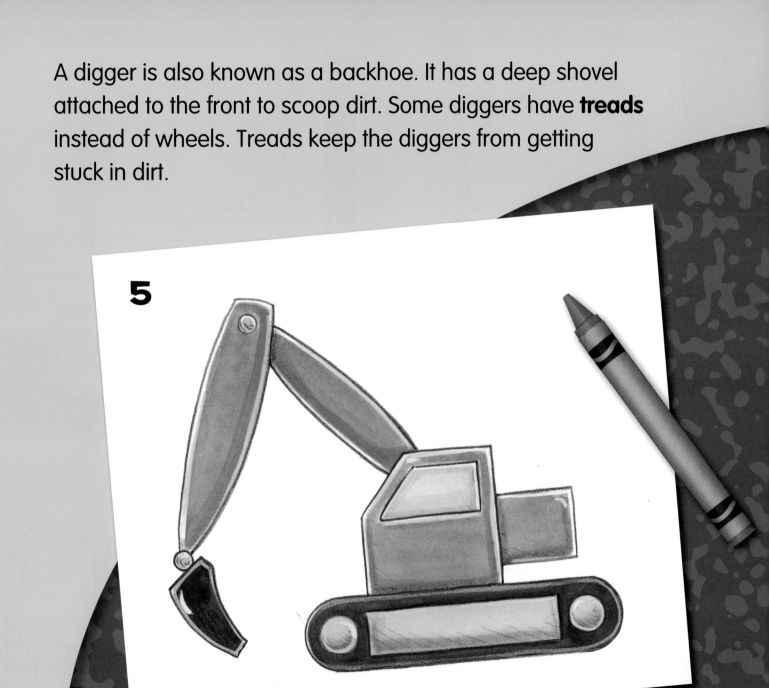

1

2

3

4

CONCRETE MIXER

A concrete mixer has a rounded tank. This is where the concrete is mixed and stored. The mixer also has a slide for pouring the wet concrete when it is ready.

5

1

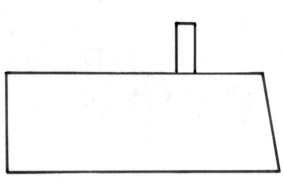

2

TRACTOR

3

4

There are many kinds of tractors. They come in a lot of colors. Tractors can be green, black, red, or blue. Tractors often have small front wheels and big back wheels.

5

1

2

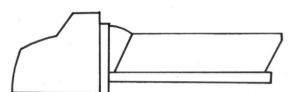

BIG RIG WITH SIDE DUMP

3

4

A big rig with side dump is an 18-wheeler. It has a large bucket in the back. It tips to the side to dump out sand or dirt.

5

1

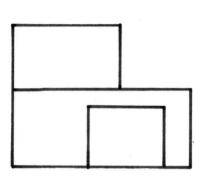

2

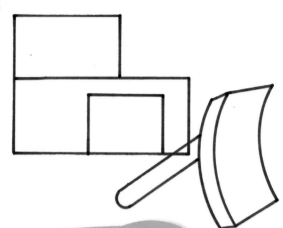

BULLDOZER

3

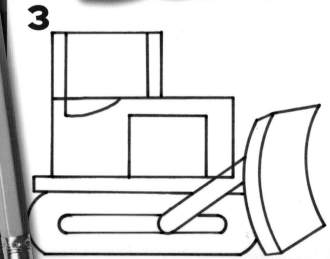

4

A bulldozer has a big metal plate in front that can push things around. Instead of wheels, a bulldozer has metal treads.

5

1

2

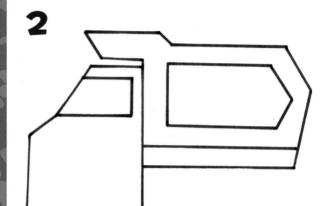

DUMP TRUCK

3

4

A big rig with side dump is an 18-wheeler. It has a large bucket in the back. It tips to the side to dump out sand or dirt.

1

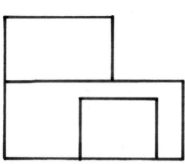

2

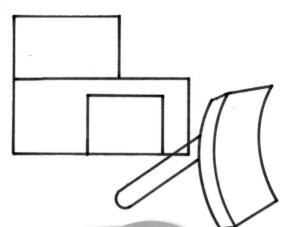

BULLDOZER

3

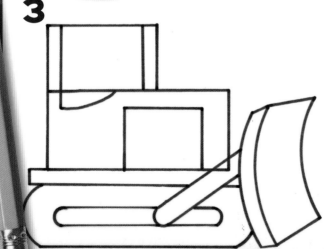

4

A dump truck has an empty bucket on its back. This large bucket can carry heavy loads. The bucket tilts back to dump the load.

5

1

2

CRANE

3

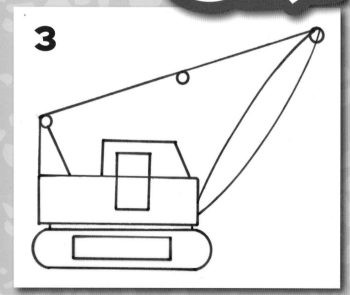

4

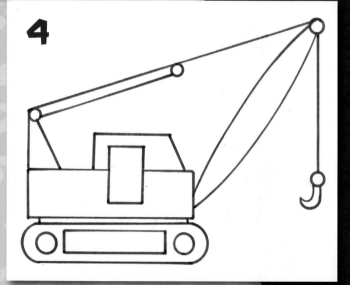

A crane is named after the bird with the same name. The bird has a very long neck. The machine has a long arm. A crane has a hook at the end of the arm that picks things up.

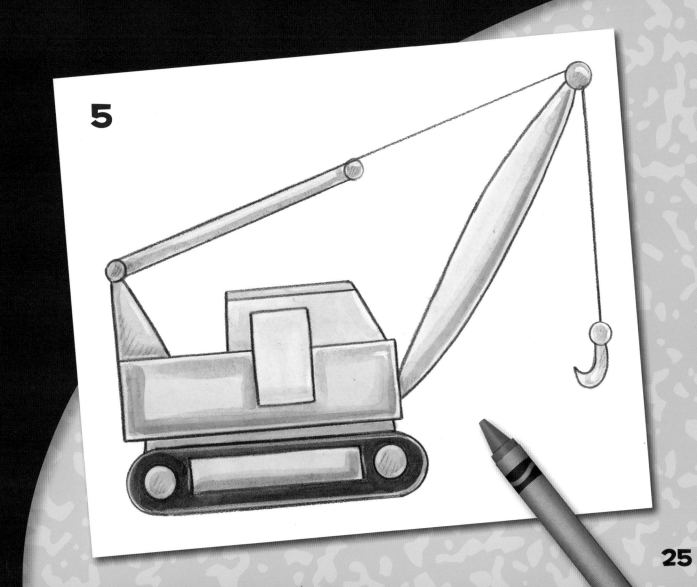

5

1

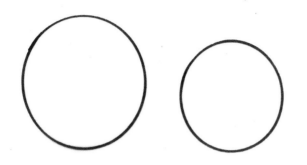

2

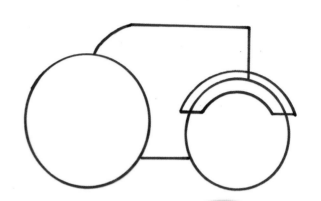

STEAMROLLER

3

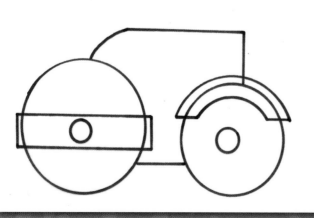

4

A steamroller has a heavy roller at its front. It may have a roller at the back end of the machine, too. The rollers make a road flat and smooth.

5

MORE DRAWING

Now you know how to draw machines at work. Here are some ways to keep drawing them.

Machines at work come in different shapes and sizes. You can draw them all! Try using pens or colored pencils to draw and color in details. Experiment with crayons and markers to give your drawings different colors and textures. You can also paint your drawings. Watercolors are easy to use. If you make a mistake, you can wipe it away with a damp cloth. Try tracing the outline of your drawing with a crayon or a marker. Then paint over it with watercolor. What happens?

Drawing Real Machines at Work

When you want something new to draw, look around. There might be a construction site nearby. Once you find one, pick a machine to draw. Look at the machine carefully. Does it have wheels or treads? What color is it? Does it have a bucket, arm, or shovel? Now try drawing it! If you need help, use the examples in this book to guide you.

GLOSSARY

concrete (KON-kreet): Concrete is a building material made of sand, gravel, cement, and water. Concrete mixers store concrete in their tanks.

construction sites (kun-STRUK-shun SYTS): Construction sites are places where things are being built or worked on. Big machines are usually needed at construction sites.

pave (PAYV): To pave means to cover a road with a hard material, such as concrete. Steamrollers help pave a road.

rubble (RUB-ul): Rubble is broken stones, wood, and bricks. Diggers scoop up rubble.

treads (TREDS): Treads are the ridged tracks on a machine. Treads keep a digger from getting stuck.

FIND OUT MORE

BOOKS

Coppendale, Jean, and Ian Graham. *The Great Big Book of Mighty Machines*. Buffalo, NY: Firefly Books, 2009.

Emberley, Ed. *Ed Emberley's Drawing Book: Make a World*. New York: Little Brown, 2006.

Love, Carrie, and Lorrie Mack. *I Can Draw Machines*. New York: DK, 2006.

WEB SITES

Visit our Web site for links about drawing machines at work:

childsworld.com/links

Note to Parents, Teachers, and Librarians: We routinely verify our Web links to make sure they are safe and active sites. So encourage your readers to check them out!

INDEX

ABOUT THE AUTHOR:
Susan Kesselring loves children, books, nature, and her family. She teaches K-1 students in a progressive charter school in Castle Rock, Minnesota.

ABOUT THE ILLUSTRATOR:
Susan DeSantis is a freelance children's book illustrator. She lives in Westerly, Rhode Island, with her husband and children. The art for this book was done in gouache and colored pencils on pressed watercolor paper.